# Tractors

By Hal Rogers

SCHOLASTIC INC.

New York   Toronto   London   Auckland   Sydney
Mexico City   New Delhi   Hong Kong   Buenos Aires

For information regarding permission, write to:
The Child's World®, Inc.
P.O. Box 326
Chanhassen, Minnesota 55317

Photos: © 1999 David M. Budd Photography

ISBN 0-439-65049-6

Printed in the U.S.A.
First Scholastic printing, February 2004

# Contents

# On the Job

On the job, farmers use tractors to

work in their fields.

This tractor has a big **blade** on the front of it. The farmer uses the blade to push things out of the way.

The blade can push animal **feed** into

a neat pile. If it snows, the blade can

push snow off roads, too.

Some tractors have big wheels.

Other tractors have **crawler tracks.**

The wheels and crawler tracks

help tractors move across rough,

bumpy fields.

A tractor can pull heavy machines, such as a **plow.** A plow helps get **soil** ready for planting.

A tractor can also pull a **trailer.**

Trailers can carry **grain** from the field to a **silo.**

Farmers have used tractors for many years. Today's tractors look very different from older ones.

# Climb Aboard!

Do you want to see where the farmer sits? The field is very dusty. The **cab** protects the farmer from dust. The farmer uses a steering wheel to drive the tractor. The farmer uses **controls** to run machines that the tractor pulls.

# Up Close

## The inside

1. The steering wheel

2. The controls

3. The driver's seat

# The outside

1. The blade

2. The wheels

3. The cab

4. The crawler tracks

# Glossary

**blade** (BLAYD)
A blade is a sharp metal tool on the front of a tractor. A blade pushes things out of the way.

**cab** (KAB)
A cab is where a farmer sits to drive a tractor. A cab has a seat, a steering wheel, and controls.

**controls** (kun-TROLZ)
Controls are tools that are used to help make something work. A farmer uses controls to run the machines that a tractor pulls.

**crawler tracks** (KRAWL-er TRAX)
Crawler tracks are huge belts that run around and around to move a machine back and forth. Some tractors have crawler tracks.

**feed** (FEED)
Feed is food for animals. A tractor blade can push feed into a pile.

**grain** (GRAYN)
Grain is food that comes from the seeds of grassy plants. Grain provides food for people and animals.

**plow** (PLOW)
A plow is a machine that can be pulled by a tractor. A plow turns soil over and breaks it up.

**silo** (SY-loh)
A silo is a tall, cylindrical building on a farm. Farmers store grain or feed in silos.

**soil** (SOYL)
Soil is the dirt in a field or garden. A plow gets soil ready for planting.

**trailer** (TRAY-ler)
A trailer is a vehicle that is used to carry things. A trailer can be pulled by a tractor or other vehicle.